Fair Shares

FRACTIONS

T E R C

Investigations in Number, Data, and Space®

Dale Seymour Publications®

Menlo Park, California

The *Investigations* curriculum was developed at TERC (formerly
Technical Education Research Centers) in collaboration with Kent State
University and the State University of New York at Buffalo. The work was
supported in part by National Science Foundation Grant No. ESI-9050210.
TERC is a nonprofit company working to improve mathematics and science
education. TERC is located at 2067 Massachusetts Avenue, Cambridge,
MA 02140.

This project was supported, in part,
by the
National Science Foundation
Opinions expressed are those of the authors
and not necessarily those of the Foundation

Managing Editor: Catherine Anderson
Series Editor: Beverly Cory
Manuscript Editor: Karen Becker
ESL Consultant: Nancy Sokol Green
Production/Manufacturing Director: Janet Yearian
Production/Manufacturing Coordinator: Barbara Atmore
Design Manager: Jeff Kelly
Design: Don Taka
Illustrations: Jane McCreary, Carl Yoshihara
Composition: Archetype Book Composition

This book is published by Dale Seymour Publications®, an imprint of
Addison Wesley Longman, Inc.

Dale Seymour Publications
2725 Sand Hill Road
Menlo Park, CA 94025
Customer Service: 800-872-1100

Order number DS43859
ISBN 1-57232-712-X
16 17 18 19 20-ML-06 05 04 03

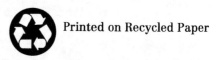

Printed on Recycled Paper

Contents

---

*Repeated-use sheet

Sharing One Brownie (page 1 of 2)

Cut up large brownie rectangles and glue the pieces below. Show how you would make fair shares.

1. 2 people share a brownie. Each person gets $\boxed{\dfrac{1}{2}}$.

2. 4 people share a brownie. Each person gets $\boxed{\phantom{\dfrac{1}{2}}}$.

3. 8 people share a brownie. Each person gets $\boxed{\phantom{\dfrac{1}{2}}}$.

Sharing One Brownie (page 2 of 2)

4. 3 people share a brownie. Each person gets ☐ .

5. 6 people share a brownie. Each person gets ☐ .

Different-Shaped Pieces

Here is a picture of a brownie cut into four pieces:

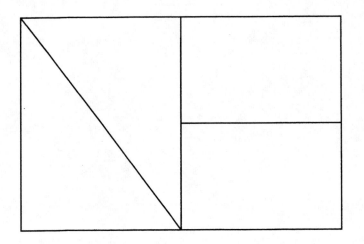

Some people think these are not fair shares.
Write what you believe.

I believe that the rectangle pieces and the triangle
pieces _____ the same size because
　　　　　are/are not

_____

_____

_____

_____

_____

_____

_____

_____

_____

HOW TO MAKE FRACTION CARDS

Materials: 5 sheets of paper (all the same color), a pen or crayon, scissors

What to Do

Fold and label sheets as shown. Write each fraction on one side only. Mark the fold lines. Cut on the lines.

Halves Fold the sheet in the middle.

Thirds Fold the sheet in 3 equal pieces.

Fourths Fold the sheet in half one way, then in half the other way, to make 4 equal pieces.

Sixths Fold the sheet the way you did to make thirds. Cut apart the thirds. Fold two of the thirds in half and cut to make long, skinny sixths. Cut the other third in half the other way to make chunky sixths.

Eighths Fold the sheet into fourths. Open the paper to see the folds. Fold each fourth in half.

Store your Fraction Cards in a plastic bag or envelope. Save these directions with them. You may want to make another set for playing games.

Ideas to Try at Home

Turn over the cards to hide the labels. Order the cards from smallest to largest. Then turn them over. Look at the number pattern. What do you see?

Find different combinations to make one whole. Put the Fraction Cards on top of a whole piece of paper to keep track. Keep a list of your combinations. For example:

$$\frac{1}{2} + \frac{1}{3} + \frac{1}{6} = 1 \qquad\qquad \frac{1}{3} + \frac{1}{3} + \frac{1}{3} = 1$$

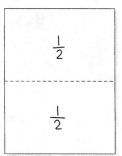
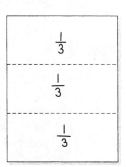
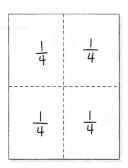
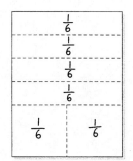
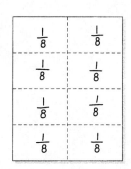

To the Family

How to Make Fraction Cards

Sessions 1–2

Math Content
Dividing rectangles into equal parts to make a set of Fraction Cards

Materials
How to Make Fraction Cards
5 sheets of colored paper (all the same color)
Small envelope or plastic bag
Pen or Crayon
Scissors

In class, students have been using paper rectangles and Fraction Cards to explore fractions and figure out which fractions are equal. For homework, your child will make a second set of Fraction Cards to keep and use at home. Ask your child how to make a set, or refer to the sheet How to Make Fraction Cards, for directions. Later in this unit, your child will use the Fraction Cards to play some fraction games, so please store them in a safe place.

Sharing Several Brownies

_____ brownies shared by _____ people
number of brownies   number of people

One person's share is _____.

Sharing Several Brownies

_____ brownies shared by _____ people
number of brownies   number of people

One person's share is _____.

Sharing Several Brownies

_____ brownies shared by _____ people

number of brownies   number of people

One person's share is _____.

Sharing Several Brownies

_____ brownies shared by _____ people
number of brownies   number of people

One person's share is _____.

15

Naming Fraction Shares

1. In these brownie pictures, one person's share
    is the shaded part.

    a. How much brownie is this share?

    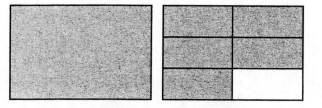

    b. How much brownie is this share?

2. Three students did this problem:

    They got three different answers
    for one person's share.

    All of their answers are correct.

    How can that be?

    Make drawings to show that at
    least two of these answers are
    the same.

3 people sharing 5 brownies
Anne: $1\frac{2}{3}$
Rachel: 1 and $\frac{1}{2}$ and $\frac{1}{6}$
Carl: $\frac{5}{3}$

To the Family

Naming Fraction Shares

Sessions 3–4

Math Content
Dividing rectangles into equal parts
Combining fractions

Materials
Student Sheet 4
Pencil

In class, students have been dividing rectangles into equal parts, or "fair shares." They have been identifying fractional parts and combining those with unlike denominators to make a whole. For homework, your child will complete Student Sheet 4. We will be discussing this work in class, so please help your child remember to bring it back to school.

Hexagon Cookies

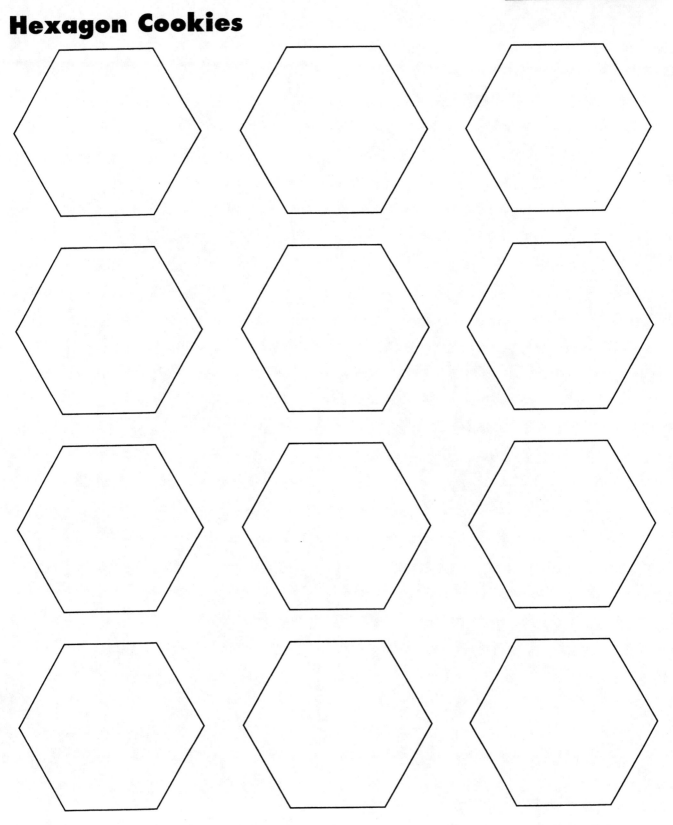

Use pattern blocks. Show all the ways to make 1 whole cookie.
Have you found them all? Are any of your designs the same?

Hexagon Cookies

Use pattern blocks. Show all the ways to make 1 whole cookie.
Have you found them all? Are any of your designs the same?

Many Ways to Make a Share

Think of sharing brownies or hexagon cookies.
Write all the fractions you know that work.

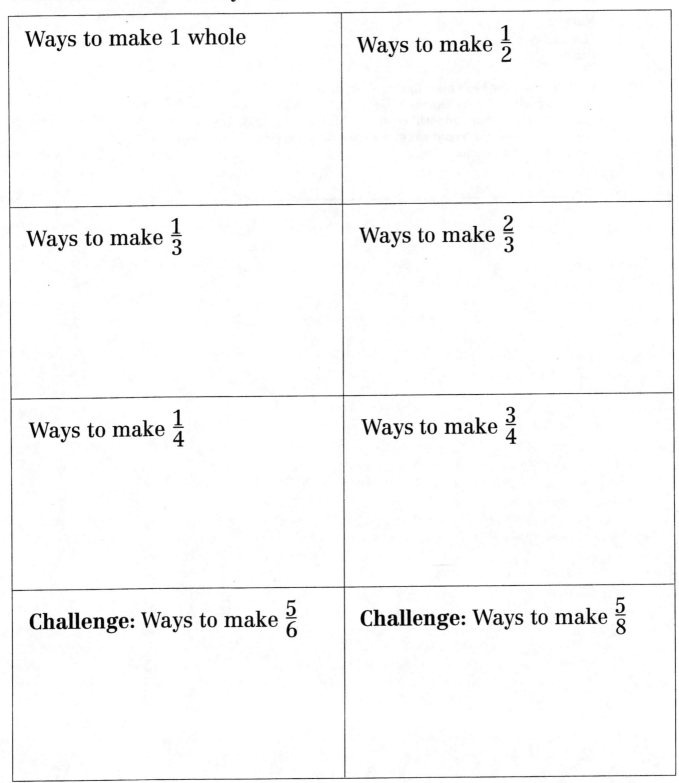

Ways to make 1 whole	Ways to make $\frac{1}{2}$
Ways to make $\frac{1}{3}$	Ways to make $\frac{2}{3}$
Ways to make $\frac{1}{4}$	Ways to make $\frac{3}{4}$
Challenge: Ways to make $\frac{5}{6}$	**Challenge:** Ways to make $\frac{5}{8}$

To the Family

Many Ways to Make a Share

Sessions 1–2

Math Content
Identifying fractional parts that are equal
Writing fractions

Materials
Student Sheet 6
Pencil

In class, students have been finding and recording fractions that are equal to each other, for example, $1/4 + 1/4 = 1/2$ and $1/3 + 1/6 = 1/2$. For homework, your child will continue this work on Student Sheet 6. Share your ideas with your child, who has been asked to record those that make sense to him or her.

Who Gets the Larger Share? (page 1 of 2)

1. Group A: 3 people share 5 brownies.
   Group B: 2 people share 5 brownies.

   Who gets the larger share? _____
   Tell how you decided. Use words or drawings or both.

2. Group C: 6 people share 4 brownies.
   Group D: 3 people share 2 brownies.

   Who gets the larger share? _____
   Tell how you decided. Use words or drawings or both.

Who Gets the Larger Share? (page 2 of 2)

3. Group E: 3 people share 4 cookies.
   Group F: 2 people share 3 cookies.

   Who gets the larger share? _____
   Tell how you decided. Use words or drawings or both.

4. Group G: 3 people share 8 cookies.
   Group H: 2 people share 7 cookies.

   Who gets the larger share? _____
   Tell how you decided. Use words or drawings or both.

Letter to a Second Grader

Some people think 1 and $\frac{1}{4}$ is a larger share than 1 and $\frac{1}{3}$.

Some people think 1 and $\frac{1}{3}$ is a larger share than 1 and $\frac{1}{4}$.

Which share do you think is bigger?
Write a letter to a second grader. Tell why you are right.
Use drawings to explain your thinking.
Remember, a second grader must understand what you write.

Hexagon Cookies

Use pattern blocks. Show all the ways to make 1 whole cookie.
Have you found them all? Are any of your designs the same?

Hexagon Cookies

Use pattern blocks. Show all the ways to make 1 whole cookie.
Have you found them all? Are any of your designs the same?

How to Play the Fraction Card Game

Materials: 2 sets of Fraction Cards

Players: 2 (or two teams of 2)

How to Play

1. This game requires some space, so try to play on the floor or find a table that is clear. Each player starts with a full set of Fraction Cards that are mixed up. Turn the cards so the fraction labels are face down.

2. Both players turn up one card at a time from the top of their sets, showing the fraction label.

   The player who turns up the card with the bigger fraction takes both cards (like in the card game War). If both cards show the same size fraction, both players turn up another card. The player with the bigger fraction takes all four cards.

3. Each time you win cards, try to make a whole with them. You may use any cards you have already won.

   For example, you could make some wholes out of halves, thirds, and sixths. You could make other wholes out of halves, fourths, and eighths.

   Other combinations will also work together, such as 2 fourths and 3 sixths. Leave your wholes out on the table.

4. Continue taking turns and making wholes until you have used up all the cards. The person with the most wholes at the end wins the game.

To the Family

How to Play the Fraction Card Game

Session 4

Math Content
Comparing fractions
Combining fractions that equal one

Materials
Student Sheet 9
2 sets of Fraction Cards

In class, we have been playing two fraction games: the Fraction Cookie Game and the Fraction Card Game. Tonight for homework, your child will teach the Fraction Card Game to someone at home. Ask your child how to play, or refer to Student Sheet 9 for directions.

In order to play, each player will need a set of Fraction Cards. Your child has brought home the set that she or he has made at school, and, hopefully, you still have the one that was made for homework. If not, you and your child can easily make another one.

How Many Altogether?

1. Isaac had a birthday party. He baked large cookies for himself and five friends. After the six people at the party shared all the cookies evenly, each person had 1 and $\frac{1}{3}$ cookies.

   How many cookies did Isaac bake altogether? Show your work here or on the back.

2. Four friends shared some brownies evenly. Each person got a whole brownie and one-fourth of another brownie.

   How many brownies did the friends start with? Show your work.

3. Three friends shared some cookies. They each got two cookies and two-thirds of a cookie.

   How many cookies did they have altogether? Show your work.

Challenge Problem

A group of friends had some cookies that they shared evenly. Each person got one and a half cookies.

How many cookies do you think they might have started with? How many people might have been in the group?

Number of people	Number of cookies

More Backward Sharing

Solve each problem. Write about your thinking or
use a drawing to show your solution.

1. Two brothers shared some brownies with two
   friends. They each got two whole brownies
   and $\frac{1}{4}$ of another. How many brownies did they
   start with?

2. Four friends and two teachers shared some
   brownies at a class picnic. They each got one
   whole brownie and $\frac{1}{3}$ of another. How many
   brownies did they start with?

3. Make up your own backward sharing problem.
   Show your work on the back of this sheet.

To the Family

More Backward Sharing

Sessions 5–6

Math Content

Solving problems that involve thinking about fractional parts in
relation to a whole

Materials

Student Sheet 11
Fraction Cards
Pencil

In class, students have been solving problems in which the givens are
the number of people sharing something and the fractional amount each
person gets; students have to figure out how many whole items there
were to start with. For example, If six people each got half a brownie,
how many whole brownies were there to start with? This is a reversal of
the more typical problem, If six people need to share three brownies,
how much does each person get? Tonight for homework, you child will
solve some "backward sharing" problems and then make up a new one.
Fraction Cards may be a useful tool for solving these problems.

To the Family

Mystery Fractions

Session 7

Math Content
Making designs that have a certain fraction of one color

Materials
Triangle paper
Markers, crayons, or pencils in four colors (red, blue, yellow, green)

In class, students have been using triangle paper to make designs that are half yellow. This can be challenging because as new parts are added to the design, the size of the whole and of each fractional part changes. You might explore these issues with your child on the extra piece of triangle paper. Tonight for homework, your child will draw a design with a specific fractional part colored yellow and record the fraction that is yellow on the back. Other people can then try to guess what the mystery fraction is.

TRIANGLE PAPER

To the Family

Mystery Fractions

Session 7

Math Content
Making designs that have a certain fraction of one color

Materials
Triangle paper
Markers, crayons, or pencils in four colors (red, blue, yellow, green)

In class, students have been using triangle paper to make designs that are half yellow. This can be challenging because as new parts are added to the design, the size of the whole and of each fractional part changes. You might explore these issues with your child on the extra piece of triangle paper. Tonight for homework, your child will draw a design with a specific fractional part colored yellow and record the fraction that is yellow on the back. Other people can then try to guess what the mystery fraction is.

Other Things to Share

1. How would you share each of the following?
   Write about your thinking or use a drawing
   to show your solution.

    9 brownies shared among 4 people

   9 balloons shared among 4 people

2. How much money does each person get?
   Compare your answer to the answer you get
   using a calculator.

    9 dollars shared among 4 people

   9 ÷ 4 on a calculator

3. Put a circle around each of your four answers above.
   They are all answers to 4 people sharing 9 things.

   How are they different from each other?
   How are they alike?

Sharing With and Without
a Calculator (page 1 of 2)

1. When 2 people share 3 brownies, what is
   each person's fair share?

   One person's share: _____   Calculator answer: _____

2. Make up a sharing problem so that each
   person gets one-half.

   _____ people share _____

   One person's share: $\frac{1}{2}$ Calculator answer: _____

3. Explain why 1.5 stands for the same amount
   that the fraction $1\frac{1}{2}$ does.

   _____

   _____

   _____

   _____

   _____

Sharing With and Without
a Calculator (page 2 of 2)

4. When 4 people share 5 brownies, what is each person's fair share?

One person's share: _____   Calculator answer: _____

5. Make up a sharing problem so that each person gets one-fourth.

_____ people share _____

One person's share: $\frac{1}{4}$ Calculator answer: _____

6. What fraction is 0.25 equal to?

How would you explain to a friend why the two amounts are equal?

_____

_____

_____

_____

More Money Sharing Problems

Solve each problem. Use the space at the right or the back of this sheet to write about your thinking or draw to show your solution.

1. Imagine that you and a friend had 3 dollars to share equally. How much money would each of you get?

_____

2. What if you and 3 friends had 6 dollars to share equally? How much money would each of you get?

_____

3. **Challenge:** If 3 people had 10 dollars to share equally, how much money would each person get?

To the Family

More Money Sharing Problems

Sessions 1–2

Math Content
Solving problems that relate fractions to both division and decimals

Materials
Student Sheet 14
Pencil

In class, students have been thinking about how they might share different kinds of things among groups of people. Some things we have explored can be shared exactly (2 brownies among 4 people), while other cannot (2 balloons among 3 people). Still others are dependent upon the situation (1 dollar can be split evenly among 4 people but not among 3). For homework, your child will solve more problems about sharing money and record his or her work on Student Sheet 14.

More Sharing Problems

Solve each problem. Use writing and drawings to show your solution.

1. Find $\frac{1}{5}$ of 100 pattern blocks so that 5 children can share the blocks equally.

_____

2. Find $\frac{1}{4}$ of 32 crayons to show how many crayons each of 4 students could have.

_____

3. Make up your own sharing problem. Show your work on the back of this sheet.

To the Family

More Sharing Problems

Session 3

Math Content
Solving problems that relate fractions ($1/3$ of 20) and division ($20 \div 3$)

Materials
Student Sheet 15
Pencil
Objects for counting (optional)

In class, students have been solving problems that relate fractions and division, for example, finding $1/3$ of 22 peanuts to show how many peanuts each of 3 people would get. For homework, your child will continue solving these kinds of problems on Student Sheet 15 and then make up a new one.

The Arranging Chairs Puzzle

What You Will Need

30 small objects to use as chairs (for example, cubes, blocks, tiles, chips, pennies, buttons)

What to Do

1. Choose a number greater than 30.

2. Figure out all the ways you can arrange that many chairs. Each row must have the same number of chairs. Your arrangements will make rectangles of different sizes.

3. Write down the dimensions of each rectangle you make.

4. Choose another number and start again. Be sure to make a new list of dimensions for each new number.

Example
All the ways to arrange 12 chairs

Dimensions
1 by 12
12 by 1
2 by 6
6 by 2
3 by 4
4 by 3

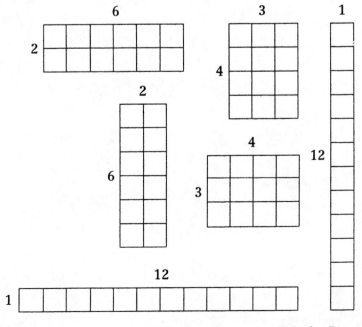

Practice Page A

I have a total of 98¢ in my pockets. I have 3 dimes,
5 nickels, and 2 pennies in one pocket. How much
do I have in the other pocket?

Show how you solved this problem. You can use
numbers, words, or pictures.

Practice Page B

I have 68¢. I put half the money in one pocket
and half the money in the other pocket. How much
money did I put in one pocket?

Show how you solved this problem. You can use
numbers, words, or pictures.

Practice Page C

In our classroom, we have 2 bookcases. Each bookcase has 4 shelves. On each shelf, there are 10 books. How many books do we have in our classroom?

Show how you solved this problem. You can use numbers, words, or pictures.

Practice Page D

I bought 3 cartons of eggs. Each carton had 8 eggs.
How many eggs did I buy?

Show how you solved this problem. You can use
numbers, words, or pictures.